# introduction

The Human Rights Act is an exciting and important piece of legislation that affects us all. However, it's written in complex legal language and needs to be translated into everyday language that we can all understand.

**This booklet, the Easy Guide to the Human Rights Act, aims to:**

- Make people think about their rights in relation to the Human Rights Act

- Empower people with learning disabilities to challenge the status quo where upholding rights may not always be a priority

- Encourage staff, carers and others to assist in promoting individual human rights

- Help others to talk about rights and wrongs.

The booklet and poster were produced by a group of people with learning disabilities and others at Working with Words, together with Andrea Hughes, a psychologist from Oxleas NHS Trust.

They are guides, not legal documents, although they have been checked by an international human rights lawyer and a lawyer specialising in learning disabilities.

People with learning disabilities must speak up for their rights. Staff employed by public bodies must enforce human rights. This guide will help this new rights culture to take hold and flourish.

## contributors

**Keith Aubrey**

**Donna Ferguson**

**Hirbai Halai**

**Elaine Hurault**

**Claire Jones**

**Ciciline Moseley**

**Mark Padmore**

**Cassy Price**

1

# who should use this guide?

This guide has been written for staff, carers and anyone involved in helping people with learning disabilities. The guide will be useful for:

- Staff in day, residential and care services

- Parents and carers

- Teachers and educationalists working with people with learning disabilities

- Clinicians and medical staff

- Advocates and self help groups

- Voluntary agencies

- Anyone wanting to know more about the Human Rights Act

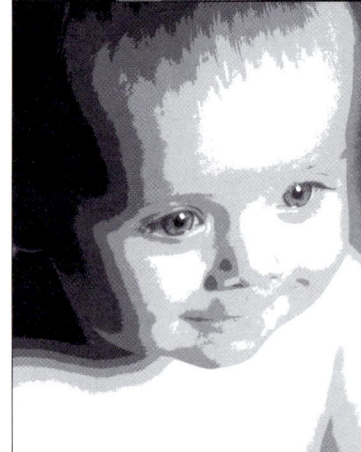

# how to use this guide

In the booklet there are a number of scenarios and stories for discussion. These stories are based on real life events raised by some members of the Working with Words group. The opening phrases have been used with permission although the stories that follow are made up. There are suggestions for action underneath each story. Each story illustrates common examples of human rights abuses experienced by the group. There are others and staff need to be aware of these.

After the scenarios section there are more practical tips and advice and a list of contact names and numbers for more support.

The guide has a poster that you can pull out and display in your day centre, residential home, office or club.

The poster has both 'rights' and 'wrongs' illustrated with practical examples. Next to each statement on the poster there is the letter A and a number. This represents the relevant Article of the Human Rights Act.

The guide has a poster that you can pull out and display in your day centre, residential home, office or club.

# the human rights act

The Human Rights Act came into force in this country on 2 October 2000. It brings the rights outlined in the European Convention of Human Rights into English law for the first time.

## The new law means that:

- It is unlawful for a public authority, such as a government department, local authority or the police, to breach the European Convention on Human Rights unless an Act of Parliament meant that the authority had no other choice.

- People can take their case to a UK court or tribunal. Before, people who felt their human rights were being ignored had to go to the European Court of Human Rights in Strasbourg. This was often expensive and slow.

- All new UK laws must fit in with the Human Rights Act. If this is not possible, Parliament will decide what to do.

In the past it was relatively easy for people with learning disabilities to be put away in institutions and denied their freedom, dignity and respect. We are optimistic that the Human Rights Act will make it easier to challenge abuses of human rights in the future.

The Human Rights Act will not address all wrongs and it is not yet clear how the new Act will be used. For example, human rights abuses by private individuals may be challenged under the Human Rights Act but this is very complex. The Act *is* designed to protect individuals from abuse by state institutions and people working for these institutions. A better understanding of human rights should ensure that individual rights are incorporated into practice as a matter of course.

*The* **Human Rights Act** *became law in Britain on 2 October 2000*

# what does it say?

The Articles and Protocols of the Human Rights Act cover some of the following rights and freedoms. Articles and Protocols are legal statements, explaining the different rights contained in the Act. These are the most important ones for people with learning disabilities:

**Protocol 1, Article 1**

No one has the right to unlawfully interfere with your possessions

**Protocol 1, Article 2**

Right to access to education

| | |
|---|---|
| **Article 2** | The right to life |
| **Article 3** | No torture, inhuman or degrading treatment |
| **Article 4** | No slavery or forced labour |
| **Article 5** | The right to liberty and personal freedom |
| **Article 6** | The right to a fair trial |
| **Article 7** | No punishment without law |
| **Article 8** | The right to privacy and family life |
| **Article 9** | Freedom of thought and religion |
| **Article 10** | Freedom of expression |
| **Article 11** | Freedom of assembly (meeting others) |
| **Article 12** | The right to marry and have a family |
| **Article 14** | Freedom from discrimination |
| **Article 17** | No one has the right to destroy or abuse rights |

The Act does have limitations. For example, it does not cover the rights to work, food or housing.

**The poster in this booklet illustrates some of the rights stated in these Articles and Protocols.**

5

# what does it mean for us?

Some laws can be difficult to understand, but we all have a responsibility to ensure that we exercise these rights properly. The difficulty remains: how can we encourage people to use these rights?

- If people with learning disabilities cannot read?

- If, as parents and carers, we do not know about our rights?

- If the Articles of the Act are not displayed in a suitable language or format for people with learning disabilities to understand?

We cannot hope to answer all of these questions in this booklet but we can try to illustrate real examples of human rights abuses that happen and have happened to members of Working with Words. Equally, we cannot hope to provide all the answers to increasing everyone's participation in upholding their rights without intensive training and support to implement the Human Rights Act.

This booklet and the poster is written in plain English. They are designed to help people who may feel intimidated by the whole concept of the Human Rights Act and the law to start thinking about their rights. It explains what you can do to make sure that people with learning disabilities do not have their rights ignored.

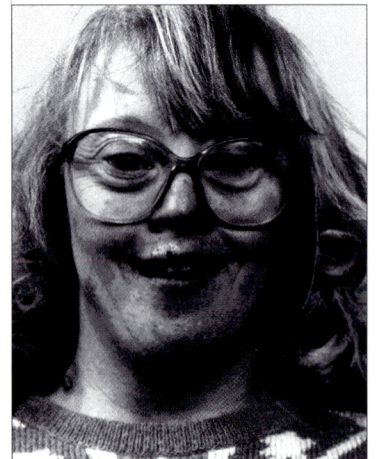

# human rights: what can go wrong?

Some people with learning disabilities in our group go to day centres, some live with their friends, others with their families. When we talked about the Human Rights Act lots of people in our group started to share very personal experiences that had upset them. Some of these experiences happened when they were in day centres and residential homes, others while they were in their family homes and in their communities.

Some people in our group have been abused, bullied, and been victims of racism. Some people have been ignored by staff or called names by children on the buses. Others were not being allowed the freedom and opportunities which the Human Rights Act encourages. Articles 3, 4 and 8 and Protocol 1, Articles 1 and 2, are most likely to be relevant to their lives.

We have used our meetings to support people, enabling them to express their views and to create something good and beneficial. All the people involved in the group have given their permission to use their stories in this booklet. They have all been offered psychological support and counselling.

Our hope is that by sharing our experiences other people with learning disabilities, their parents, carers and supporters can use this guide to identify and challenge Human Rights abuses whenever they happen.

The following stories are based on real examples, comments and stories. All the names have been changed and the scenarios are examples only.

The action and advice are intended to raise awareness of the very real issues faced by people with learning disabilities. We are not suggesting that people will necessarily win their cases against a statutory authority or service provider. Instead, we are including common scenarios that could be challenged under the Human Rights Act. If you recognise a similar situation seek expert legal advice.

**Some people in our group have been abused, bullied, and been victims of racism.**

# shared experiences of rights abuses

*'I want a job'*
*'I do work at the day centre. I get no pay for the work I do. I need a job.'*

Ben is 41 years old. He has a learning disability. He likes swimming, meeting his friends at the club and using computers. Ben has gone to the day centres on and off for 20 years. He goes to college and is learning how to get better at reading and writing. Ben's parents are getting old and he is worried about his future. He wants to learn how to live on his own or with his friends. He knows that to do this he needs a job, to help him pay his bills and look after his mum and dad.

At school and college Ben struggled but he has completed and passed training courses in cooking, food hygiene, basic skills and basic computing.

At his day centre, Ben helps the staff by answering the telephone and working in the reception area. He does this three times a week during the day and wants to get paid for the work he does. His job is busy and can be stressful in the mornings when people go out to their activities and in the evenings when they return. Ben often tells the bus drivers which person should get on the right bus and what time they are expected home. At lunch times, when the staff help people eat their lunches or are short staffed, Ben is often expected to answer the phones and takes charge of the reception area.

Ben enjoys his job but should get paid for it. Ben would like recognition and pay for the job he does.

## Action and Advice

- There are many reasons why someone may be asked to look after the reception area in a busy day centre or residential home. This is not likely to be an abuse of someone's human rights unless the individual concerned is coerced.

- As a key worker, care manager, friend or parent a person with learning disabilities may tell you that something is wrong. Questions about rights to training, education and employment could be involved.

---

**Human Rights Article?**

## Article 4

*No slavery or forced labour*

---

**What should be the terms and conditions?**

**Everyone should be paid for the work they do**

**A contract with hours worked and pay received should be offered**

**The person with learning disabilities doesn't have to carry on working unless they want to**

# shared experiences

## Scenario 2

*'I want to be with my girlfriend in my room, when we want to be together ... we're not allowed ... we have to kiss outside.'*

Kevin, 32, lives in a group home. His girlfriend, Joanne, lives in another part of the charity house and they meet at the day centre. Kevin is not allowed to have his girlfriend visit once a week. He has told staff that he would like her to visit him and would like to have private time with her in his bedroom but the staff refuse. They also open and read his letters and correspondence.

This contravenes Kevin's rights as laid down in Article 8 of the Human Rights Act. The staff are under contract to carry out public duties and therefore their actions are covered by the Act. Kevin should not be prevented from meeting anyone in private. Kevin's care manager upholds the status quo, despite his wishes, as she does not want to jeopardise the placement.

### Action and Advice

- The staff do not have a legal authority to intercept mail or deny a person privacy to conduct a personal relationship

- There may be some circumstances in which staff have to open post, for instance, if someone cannot read or needs help to keep appointments. The reasons should be agreed and given for each person

- If safety or consent issues exist the onus must be on staff to have discussed this and get agreement and permission by the resident or their legal guardian

- Decisions on privacy and personal relationships should be able to be challenged with an independent arbiter

- Complaints procedures should be accessible

- Responsibility to the service user should come first in community care packages, within resource constraints.

## Human Rights Article?

## Article 8

*The right to respect for private and family life, home and correspondence.*

# shared experiences

## Scenario 3

*'I don't like people swearing at me. We're just the same colour. Where I live, I go out to my minibus and they say 'Hello, Paki'.'*

Meera lives with her family. She likes to go out and take part in lots of activities. Meera was born in Britain. Her family are from Pakistan. Meera has a learning and physical disability. She has lots of friends at her day centre and at the college that she attends. She needs help to travel to and from her day activities.

Sometimes when Meera returns home there are a group of teenagers hanging around near Meera's house. When she gets off the minibus the teenagers shout at Meera, call her names and mock her. The council minibus driver and escort take no notice of this abuse.

When Meera's mother comes out of her house to meet Meera, Meera is often very upset by the abuse. Meera's mother does not know what to do and tries to raise the problem with the council minibus driver and escort who take no notice of this abuse.

### Action and advice

- Council employees have a duty to protect and support the people they are driving home, and they need to be more proactive to prevent this racist abuse. At the very least they should report this incident to their line manager.

- Racism is wrong; racial abuse is everyone's problem

- Help can be sought from the minibus drivers

- Someone could ring the police. The police have a new positive duty to protect individuals, particularly vulnerable adults

- Encourage the person to ignore the abuse at the time and to go home and lock their door

- Parents, carers or managers can go with the person with learning disabilities to talk to the site manager, caretaker or landlord about help

- You can talk to the anti-racist manager at the council

- You can talk to the Commission for Racial Equality.

## Human Rights Article?

### Article 8
*Protection of private and family life*

### Article 14
*No discrimination*

### Using the telephone

**Teach people with learning disabilities how to use the telephone**

**Can the person you support make 999 calls?**

**Encourage people with learning disabilities to make a card for their pocket that reminds them how to use a telephone**

# shared experiences

## Scenario 4

*'I can walk on my own indoors but I'm strapped into my wheelchair in the day centre'*

Maggie, 22, lives at home with her family and does not have any verbal communication. She arrives at her day centre by wheelchair as she cannot walk far.

Although she has a full timetable of group activities, she is strapped into her wheelchair and so cannot get about the centre on her own. On many occasions she is not participating in the activities and is positioned facing the wall away from others.

When staff are questioned about this form of restraint, it is explained as necessary because Maggie is 'spiteful'.

### Action and advice

- This scenario is wrong, bad practice and unlawful

- Maggie might be 'spiteful' but who makes a judgement about Maggie's attitude if Maggie can't verbally communicate?

- Maggie cannot communicate her complaint on her own

- Whistle blowing by other staff or visitors is a legal duty when concerns are not addressed. The Public Interest Disclosure Act 1998 provides some employment law protection for whistleblowers

- The police should be called where an offence has been committed

- Consulting a lawyer would give you advice on the legal position

- Campaign groups try to influence the government to introduce new laws

- Employees of local government, the health service, statutory bodies, associations, trusts and increasingly charities have direct responsibility for ensuring that human rights are upheld, protected and enforced.

## Human Rights Article?

## Article 3

*No torture, inhuman or degrading treatment*

# what you can do

The following are suggestions for supporting a person with learning disabilities:

- Believe the person from the start

- Help him or her practice speaking by being responsive

- Teach people to use the telephone

- Take their concerns seriously

- Talk to someone from the Community Learning Disability Team about Best Practice

- Talk to the care manager (social worker)

- Find out about rights

- Be prepared to question practices

- Remember there are rights now

- Use the poster to point out what these rights are

- Call the police in an emergency or where a serious violation of rights has occurred

- If racism is the problem speak to the council anti-racism officer

- Others are there to help – ask someone from the list at the end of the booklet

- Take legal advice

- Use the courts if you need to

*suggestions* **for supporting a person with learning disabilities**

# useful contacts and addresses

Try to resolve the problem locally first but remember there are national organisations that can help you get your rights upheld.

Encourage people with learning disabilities to tell a friend or ask someone they trust for advice.

## Helpful organisations

### Local organisations

- Key worker, social worker, doctor, nurse, teacher, advocate, Community Learning Disability Team (social workers)

- The Social Services Department:
    Manager of Services
    Outreach Team
    Council Complaints officer

- NHS Trust Complaints Departments

- Police – in an emergency call 999

- Citizens Advice Bureaux

- Community Health Council

- Local MENCAP offices

- Local Scope offices

- Law centres

- Local Citizens Advice Bureau

- Advocacy Rights Group

- Local Housing Rights Group

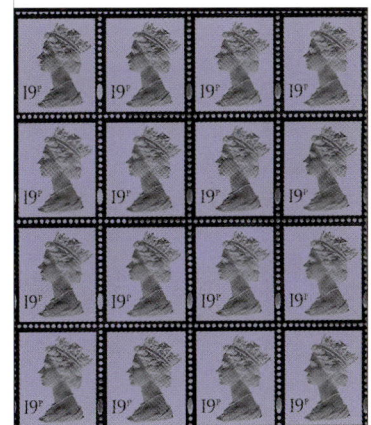

## National organisations

**Andrea Adams Trust** (advice for people being bullied) Tel: 01273 704900

**Workplace Bullying Information pack**, department GS, PO Box 67, Didcot, OX11 OYA (send large sae)

**British Institute of Learning Disabilities (BILD)**, Wolverhampton Road, Kidderminster, Worcs DY10 3PP Tel 01562 850 251

**National MENCAP**, Tel: 020 7454 0454

**People First**, Tel: 020 7485 6660

**Public Concern at Work**, Tel: 020 7404 6609

**Liberty**, 21 Tabard Street, London, Tel: 020 7403 3888, www.liberty-human-rights.org.uk

**TUC** free leaflet 'Bullied at work'. Send an sae to Congress House, London  WC1B

## For more information about the Human Rights Act

**Home Office Human Rights Unit**, Home Office, London. www.homeoffice.gov.uk/hract, 020 7273 2166

**Disability Rights Commission** Freepost MID02164, Stratford-upon-Avon, CV37 9BR Tel: 0345 622633

# staff and carers

For every right there is a corresponding duty for someone to protect those rights.

People with learning disabilities now have constitutional rights intended to prevent discrimination and unfair treatment. These rights have to be known, understood and claimed. If you work or live with someone who needs assistance to claim their rights, then it is your responsibility to assist them.

It is the law of the land. This is a new rights culture which should mean that everyone has:

- Equality before and under the law

- Equal protection

- Benefit of the law without discrimination based on race, ethnicity, colour, religion, sex, mental, physical or learning disability.

Where possible, incidents that may be covered by the Act should be resolved locally before they get to the courts. If, as a member of staff, you think there is a potential situation, do your best to resolve it immediately and then refer it to your line manager.

## Action and Advice
Consider these issues:

- Public authorities have a legal duty to act compatibly with the Act

- Can you get training and advice?

- Your professional code of conduct

- Your duty of care

- Your workplace policies

- The right to freedom of expression (Article 10) applies to everyone including employees who want to 'whisteblow'.

## And
- Speak to your supervisor or manager for advice, now

- Contact the Home Office Human Rights Taskforce (see page 14)

This is a new rights culture

# dictionary

These terms and words are used in the booklet and are not necessarily legal definitions.

**Abuse** is physical, sexual, financial or emotional harm by one person against another. It is wrong.

**Act** A body of written law.

**Articles** A legal statement, explaining the different rights contained in the Act

**Bully** Someone you think is strong or powerful does something to you, against your will. You feel bullied and you feel bad. Bullying is wrong.

**CLDT** Community Learning Disability Team.

**Complaint** What to do when you are unhappy or dissatisfied with your treatment.

**Discrimination** An act by someone, often in a position of power, against a person or group that may be seen to be different from themselves. Examples include racism, and preventing chances and opportunities to others. This is different from 'making a complaint', that is, telling someone you are unhappy or dissatisfied with your treatment.

**Duty** Obligation or responsibility.

**Equality** Treating all people fairly, providing equal chances.

**Fair** Treating all people in the same way or with some respect.

**Human Rights** Basic rights that all people should be able to enjoy, like the right to life, to be treated well and to be able to make free and independent choices.

**Injustice** Actions or events that are not right and fair. For example, the employer pays the woman less and no action is taken to stop this unfair situation.

**Justice** Actions or events that are right and fair or that make things right and fair. For example, an employer pays a woman less than a man for doing the same job; the employer is made to pay the same rates of pay.

**Laws** Laws are important rules with punishments for those who do not obey them. They are often made by government. Some are made by the United Nations (UN) or other bodies.

**Policy** A plan of action. For example, equal opportunities policies determine what a company will do to ensure the same opportunities for everybody.

**Prevent** Stop or restrain people, or deny them something.

**Protect** Defend, support, help people.

**Public authorities** Councils or governing agencies. Examples include social services, hospitals, the police, schools.

**Racism** Aggressive and blatant or less obvious bad or harmful behaviour by someone against another person or group, based on that person or group's skin colour, ethnicity or culture.

**Responsible** In charge, making sure something is done.

**Rights** Principles and rules about ways in which people should live with others.

**Unfair** Not treating people the same, and not showing respect for others

**Whistleblowing** A person who witnesses bad practice at work and reports it.

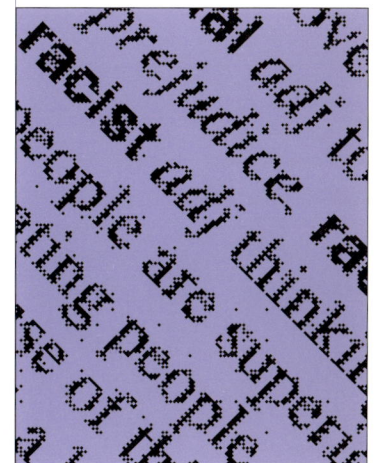

# bibliography

Liberty Briefing Paper

The Human Rights Act, 1998

Human Rights Act: Introduction, Home Office

Amnesty International Journal, 103. Sept 2000

Universal Declaration of Human Rights

'The Right to Fair and Equal Treatment, A straightforward guide to Human Rights and the Canadian HRA'. The G. Allan Roeher Institute. 1991

# who are we?

A group of us in the London Borough of Greenwich, South East London, got together to think about 'rights' and 'wrongs'. We decided that there were many things that were not right about the way some of us were treated.

We wanted to do something about how we were treated and so we looked at the new Human Rights law and decided that we could not understand it.

We decided to draft our own interpretation of the Act and use real life examples that we hope other people with learning disabilities will be able to relate to. Then we decided to create this booklet and a poster that can be displayed in day centres, residential homes and clubs to remind everyone about the Human Rights Act.

## Our Group

### Andrea Hughes

Clinical Psychologist for Oxleas NHS Trust commissioned Working with Words to create an accessible version of the Human Rights Act. Andrea has published in the areas of complaints and quality of life for people with learning disabilities, dual diagnosis and legal issues.
Andrea Hughes
Oxleas NHS Trust
Tel: 020 8319 7144

### Working with Words Ltd

Working with Words is a community business based in Woolwich in South East London. Together with our supporters we have won a number of contracts from large service providers to make their information more accessible. We are grateful to Oxleas NHS Trust for paying us to develop the poster and booklet.
Tel: 020 8855 6644
www.workingwithwords.org
Workingwith@words01.fsnet.co.uk
Phil Coombs is the manager of Working with Words Ltd

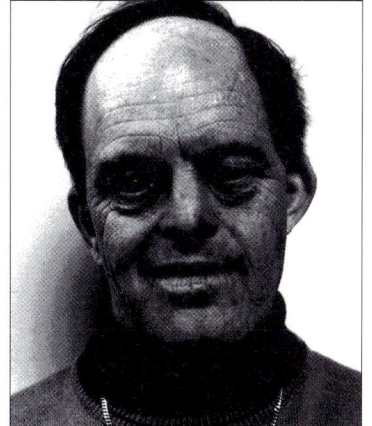

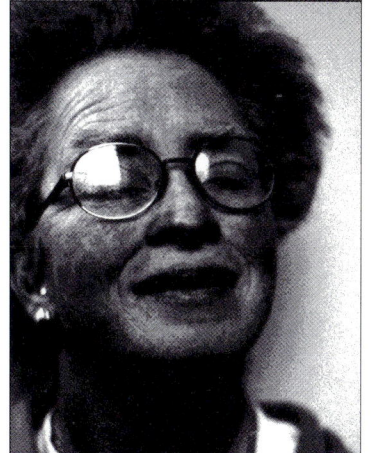

# Acknowledgements

### Speech and Language Therapy
Thanks to Elaine and Claire for their input and development

### BILD
Thank you for publishing, editing and support

### Community Care Development Centre, King's College, London
Our thanks to the CCDC for sponsoring and helping us to launch this booklet

### Professor Mike Gunn
Our thanks to Professor Mike Gunn for advising on the legal aspects of the booklet.